ASPENNE AND COLOR THE NEIGHBORHOOD

(YOUR NAME HERE)

A COLORING BOOK BY PATRICIA BELLAMY-MATHIS

Text & Illustrations Copyright © 2022 by Patricia Bellamy-Mathis
Created & designed by Patricia Bellamy-Mathis
Art by Anastasiya Rudyk
Published in 2022 by Aspenne's Library LLC, Connecticut

ISBN: 979-8-9851910-6-6

All rights reserved. No part of this book may be reproduced or transmitted in any form or by any means, electronic or mechanical, including photocopying, recording, or by any information storage and retrieval system, without the prior written permission of the author and/or publisher.

This coloring and activity book pairs best with children's book "Aspenne Colors the Neighborhood" by Patricia Bellamy-Mathis
Information for this pairing book can be found below:

Paperback ISBN: 979-8-9851910-4-2
Board Book ISBN: 979-8-9851910-5-9
Library of Congress Control Number: 2022941319

To learn more about Aspenne's Library,
visit our website at www.aspenneslibrary.com

WELCOME TO THE ASPENNE'S LIBRARY BOOK CLUB

ASPENNE'S LIBRARY
HIGHLIGHT • PROMOTE • PROVIDE
BLACK & BROWN STORIES

Hi! My name is ASPENNE

What's your name?

_____

Come along for a walk
with my family
and help us search for

COLORS

When we walk on Mondays, we look for the color

RED Fire Truck

RED Stop Sign

RED Flowers

I- spy a RED item in your home!

Draw a picture of something RED

Search for something RED in your neighborhood.

Draw what you find!

When we walk on Tuesdays,
we look for the color

I- spy a BLUE item in your home!

Draw a picture of something BLUE

Search for something BLUE in your neighborhood.

Draw what you find!

When we walk on Wednesdays, we look for the color

Yellow

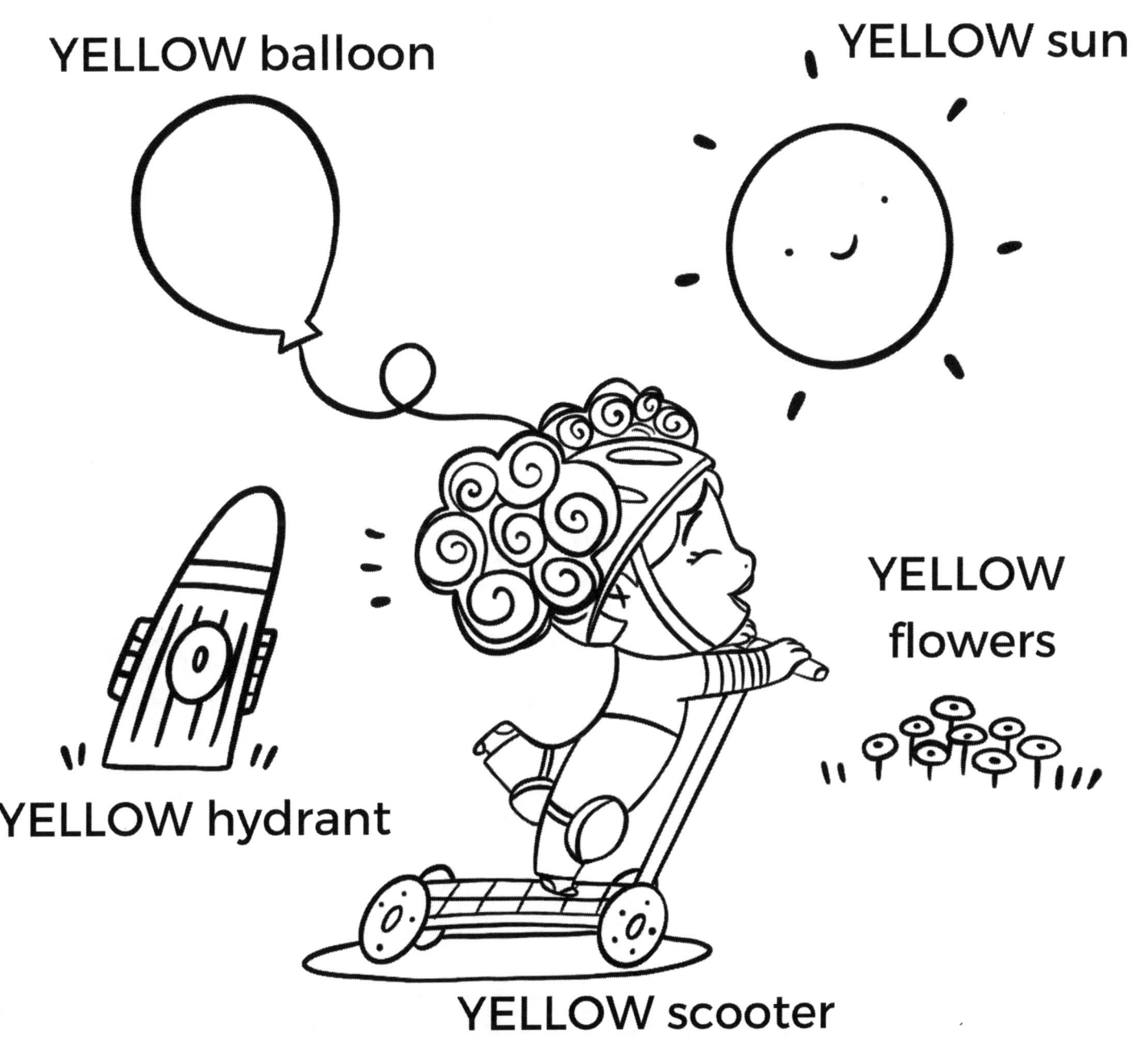

I- spy a YELLOW item in your home!

Draw a picture of something YELLOW

Search for something YELLOW in your neighborhood.

Draw what you find!

When we walk on Thursdays, we look for the color

PURPLE
umbrella

PURPLE
dog collar

PURPLE
rain coat and rain boots

I- spy a PURPLE item in your home!

Draw a picture of something PURPLE

Search for something PURPLE in your neighborhood.

Draw what you find!

I- spy a GREEN item in your home!

Draw a picture of something GREEN

Search for something GREEN in your neighborhood. Draw what you find!

When we walk on Saturdays, we look for the color ORANGE

ORANGE house

ORANGE basketball

ORANGE helmet

ORANGE bicycle

I- spy an ORANGE item in your home!

Draw a picture of something ORANGE

Search for something ORANGE in your neighborhood.

Draw what you find!

When we walk on Sundays,
we look for the colors

I- spy a BLACK item in your home!

Draw a picture of something BLACK

Search for something WHITE in your neighborhood. Draw what you find!

So excited that we could color our neighborhood together! Thank you for coming along the journey with me!

Made in the USA
Middletown, DE
04 December 2025